Paintings by Anneke Kaai
Extracts from **The Message** *by Eugene H. Peterson*

The Psalms

An Artist's Impression

InterVarsity Press
P.O. Box 1400, Downers Grove, IL 60515
World Wide Web: www.ivpress.com
E-mail: mail@ivpress.com

InterVarsity Press® is the book-publishing division of
InterVarsity Christian Fellowship/USA®, a student
movement active on campus at hundreds of
universities, colleges and schools of nursing in the
United States of America, and a member movement of
the International Fellowship of Evangelical Students.
For information about local and regional activities, write
Public Relations Dept., InterVarsity Christian
Fellowship/USA, 6400 Schroeder Rd., P.O. Box 7895,
Madison, WI 53707-7895.

All Scripture quotations, unless otherwise indicated, are
taken from The Message: Psalms by Eugene H.
Peterson. Used by permission of NavPress. All rights
reserved.

The illustration of Psalm 121:1, 2 found on page 39 is
the property of the Theological University at Apeldoorn,
The Netherlands. Reproduced with permission.

Cover illustration: "Psalm 62:1, 2" by Anneke Kaai (also
appearing on page 29)

ISBN 0-8308-2289-5

Printed and bound in Singapore.

**Library of Congress Cataloging-in-Publication Data
has been requested**.

11	10	9	8	7	6	5	4	3	2	1
08	07	06	05	04	03	02	01	00		

About the Artist

Anneke Kaai-van Wijngaarden was born in Naarden, The Netherlands, in 1951. She is married to a Dutch Reformed minister and they have two children.

After completing her initial art training at the Gooise Academy for Fine Art in the Netherlands, Anneke Kaai studied at the Gerrit Rietveld Academy in Amsterdam.

To the viewer it soon becomes clear that her work is inspired by the Bible and by her personal faith. Her paintings are quite literally "windows" to display her inspiration, which is intimately linked with her faith.

Apart from her figurative work on the Book of Revelation, the style of Anneke Kaai may be described as abstract and symbolic. A wealth of Christian images is worked into her compositions.

Her first series, on Creation, consisted of fifteen paintings, followed by a twenty-four-part series on the Book of Revelation (*Apocalypse*) painted on silk. Then there came a series of twelve works on the Ten Commandments and twelve works on the Apostolic Creed (*I Believe*), all painted on Plexiglas using oils and acrylics in combination with other materials.

The same medium was used for this present collection of paintings on the Psalms.

Previous published works by Anneke Kaai are:

- *De Schepping in Beeld* (1991, The Netherlands (NL): A. Kaai)
- *Apocalypse* (1992, Carlisle, UK: Paternoster Press)
- *Openbaring in Beeld* (3rd edition, 1997, Zoetermeer, NL: Boekencentrum)
- *I Believe* (1995, Carlisle, UK: Paternoster Press)
- *Geloof in Beeld* (1995, Zoetermeer, NL: Boekencentrum)
- *Ich bin und ich glaube* (1995, Germany and Switzerland: Brunnen-Verlag)
- *Psalmen verbeeld, a multi-media CD-ROM of images from Psalms* (1999, Ridderkerk, NL: A2M Educational Software)
- *Psalmen in Beeld* (1999, Zoetermeer, NL: Boekencentrum Mozaïek)

Anneke Kaai exhibits her work regularly in The Netherlands, often in churches where there is an increasing interest in fine art. She has also been interviewed about her work on Dutch television and her paintings are periodically featured in Dutch magazines and newspapers.

The particular verses that inspired a painting are set in bold.

Acknowledgments

Firstly thanks to my husband and children for their keen and supportive interest in my work, especially whilst painting this series, *The Psalms*.

I would also like to thank all those who helped with the editing of the text, and NavPress for their kind permission to use selections from *The Message* in this English edition.

Thanks are also due to Dolf Hoving, the photographer, for his professional touch and care in producing the high-quality transparencies necessary for reproduction of the paintings.

Finally I would like to thank my Dutch publishers, Mozaïek, for our enjoyable partnership during the preparation of this book. And I thank my English publishers, Piquant, in particular Pieter Kwant for his continued encouragement in this third English publication of my work.

I look up to the mountains;
    does my strength come from mountains?
No, my strength comes from GOD, who made heaven,
    and earth, and mountains.

              Psalm 121:1 – 2

Introduction

Throughout the ages people have been able to identify with the emotions described in the words of the Psalms, for these poems express human life in its range of joys, sorrows, and confusing doubts, all within a framework that relates to God. In my personal life too, the Psalms have played a special role; they have challenged me, comforted me and strengthened my faith. These experiences were used by the Holy Spirit as a basis for the creation of the images you see in this book.

One particular psalm, more than any other, often speaks powerfully to a person; therefore I have ended up making more than one painting of some psalms. Together the paintings in these "sets" support the strong emotions evoked by that psalm.

Dark versus light—with light often referring to God—is one characteristic feature of the paintings in this book. The dynamic movement in these compositions is far stronger and more powerful than in the works of the previous series, on the Creed. The colours, often used symbolically, are rich and vibrant here, and in some cases, stark in their contrasts. Collages are used in approximately half the works to add texture to the images. All the paintings are of an 80 to 120 size dimension and have been painted with mixed mediums on Plexiglas.

Over a period of four years I have worked with much joy on this series of twenty-five paintings. For me, painting is a Spirit-led search, struggling with the mediums, changing, adding, erasing, for that image to emerge which captures the deep emotions I experienced in response to particular Bible texts. I long that these struggling expressions may enrich you in your personal meditations on the Psalms.

Anneke Kaai
Rhenen, The Netherlands

How well God must like you—
        you don't hang out at Sin Saloon,
        you don't slink along Dead-End Road,
        you don't go to Smart-Mouth College.

Instead you thrill to GOD's Word,
        you chew on Scripture day and night.
You're a tree replanted in Eden,
        bearing fresh fruit every month,
Never dropping a leaf,
        always in blossom.

You're not at all like the wicked,
        who are mere windblown dust—
Without defense in court,
        unfit company for innocent people.

GOD charts the road you take.
The road *they* take is Skid Row.

What strikes one here is the contrast between the life with God—the ever green, abundantly fruitful tree on the right—and the life without God—the black space on the left. The tree is so vibrantly alive because it draws nourishment from the streams of water surrounding it. So too is the person who feeds day and night on the Word of God. Note how the faint scroll-like shape, representing the Law—the Torah—crosses the tree trunk, a reference to Jesus Christ.

Psalm 1

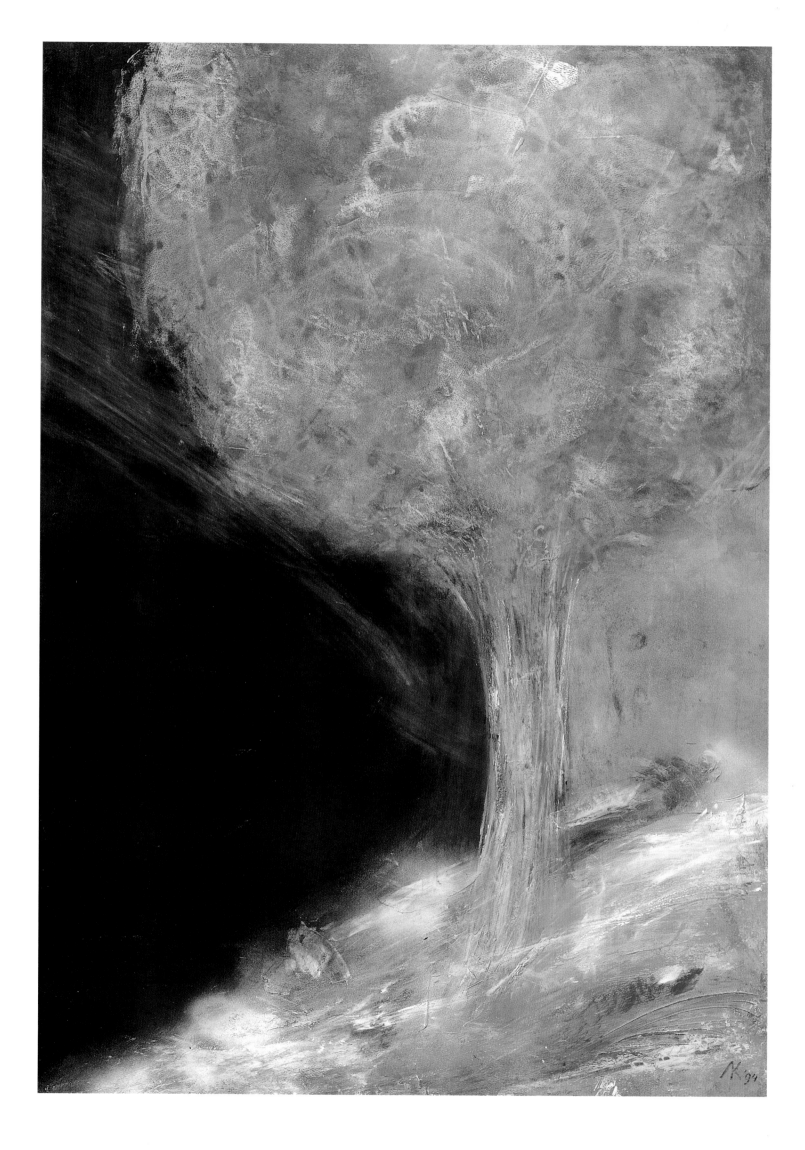

GOD, brilliant Lord,
     yours is a household name.

Nursing infants gurgle choruses about you;
     toddlers shout the songs
That drown out enemy talk,
     and silence atheist babble.

I look up at your macro-skies, dark and enormous,
     your handmade sky-jewelry,
Moon and stars mounted in their settings.
     Then I look at my micro-self and wonder,
Why do you bother with us?
     Why take a second look our way?

Yet we've so narrowly missed being gods,
     bright with Eden's dawn light.
You put us in charge of your handcrafted world,
     repeated to us your Genesis-charge,
Made us lords of sheep and cattle,
     even animals out in the wild,
Birds flying and fish swimming,
     whales singing in the ocean deeps.

GOD, brilliant Lord,
     your name echoes around the world.

Psalm 8

This psalm explores the glory of God's name as expressed in heaven and on earth. Above we see the hands of God creating the heavens, the moon and the stars. In the fingers his Hebrew name YHWH can be traced. The poet, overcome by the greatness of creation, realizes it is a miracle that God cares for an individual human being—note the relatively small size of the globe. Yet God's name is glorified on the earth where God created human beings, almost God-like, and appointed them to rule as his sovereign lords over the creatures of the land, air and sea.

Note the dominating red shapes of the question marks. Here the shape of the question mark expresses something of being bent over, burdened, weighed down with grief (tears). The light stains hint at crying out by day; the dark stains, crying out by night. But the poet finds no peace, as is seen in the restlessness of the reds—for anger—and yellows—for hatred—against a background of deep darkness. At the same time, above and to the right, light enters from the Holy One, enthroned on the praises of his people Israel whom he saved when they cried out to him in the past; and this light transforms the angry question marks into the shape of a listening ear.

God, God . . . my God!
> **Why did you dump me**
> **miles from nowhere?**
Doubled up with pain, I call to God
> **all the day long. No answer. Nothing.**
I keep at it all night, tossing and turning.

And you! Are you indifferent, above it all,
> **leaning back on the cushions of Israel's praise?**
We know you were there for our parents:
> **they cried for your help and you gave it;**
> **they trusted and lived a good life.**

And here I am, a nothing—an earthworm,
> something to step on, to squash.
Everyone pokes fun at me;
> they make faces at me, they shake their heads:
"Let's see how GOD handles this one;
> since God likes him so much,
> > let *him* help him!"

Psalm 22

In this painting, the shepherd's staff is a symbol for God. The rounded head of the staff expresses the loving care of God the Good Shepherd. When the shepherd is keeping watch, a lamb may lie down in the meadow without any cares—note the green (this colour is used to represent life) and the quiet waters. The sparkling waterfall, to the right, expresses the refreshing of the soul. When the staff is inverted, as in the lower part of this painting, the rounded crook becomes a hook. This emphasizes that when we have to pass through the dark valley— the black space below—it is God who rescues us, lifts us up, and comforts us.

GOD, my shepherd!
    I don't need a thing.
You have bedded me down in lush meadows,
    you find me quiet pools to drink from.
True to your word,
    you let me catch my breath
    and send me in the right direction.

Even when the way goes through
    Death Valley,
I'm not afraid
    when you walk at my side.
Your trusty shepherd's crook
    makes me feel secure.

You serve me a six-course dinner
    right in front of my enemies.
You revive my drooping head;
    my cup brims with blessing.

Your beauty and love chase after me
    every day of my life.
I'm back home in the house of GOD
    for the rest of my life.

Psalm 23

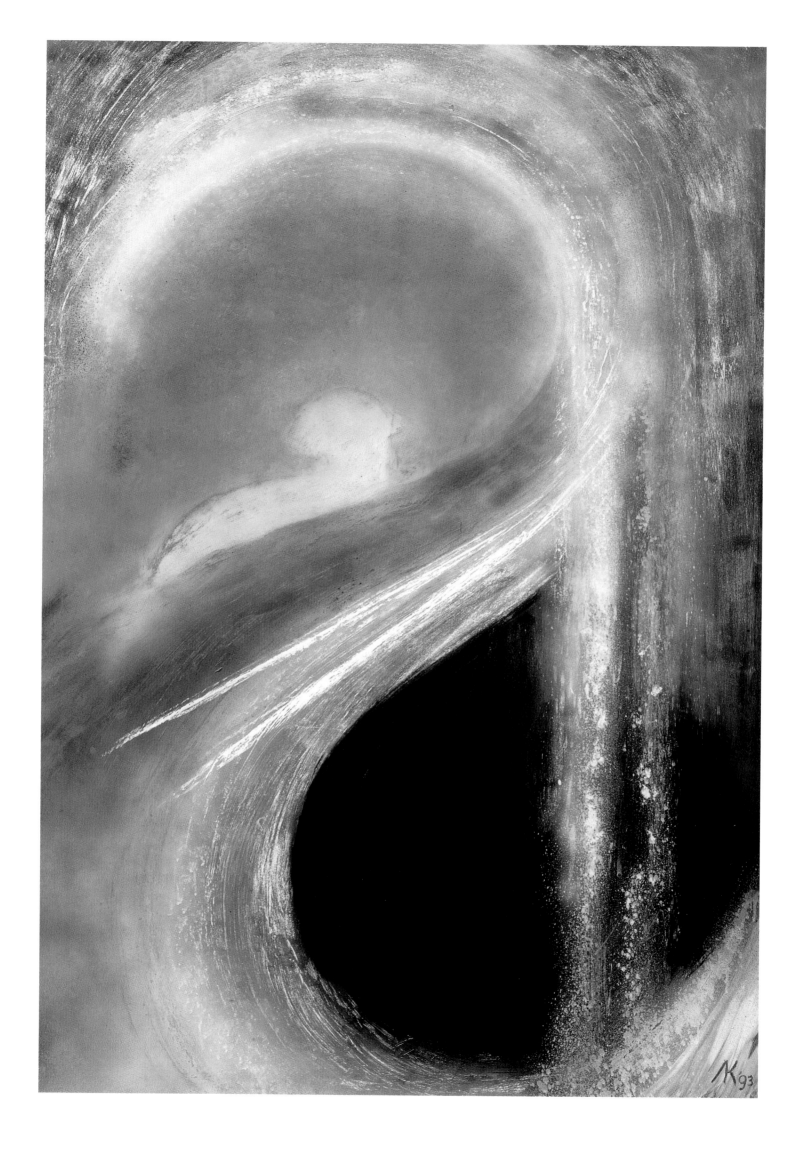

GOD claims Earth and everything in it,
    GOD claims World and all who live on it.
He built it on Ocean foundations,
    laid it out on River girders. . . .

Wake up, you sleepyhead city!
Wake up, you sleepyhead people!
    King-Glory is ready to enter.

Who is this King-Glory?
    GOD, armed
    and battle-ready.

Wake up, you sleepyhead city!
Wake up, you sleepyhead people!
    King-Glory is ready to enter.

Who is this King-Glory?
    GOD of the angel armies:
    he is King-Glory.

There is a huge, dynamic spaciousness in this work. The old gates are lifted up out of their buttresses for the Almighty King, Lord of the Heavenly Armies, to enter. A radiant three-pointed crown represents this King. The bright shape of the crown joins up with its lighter reflection to form a star—a reminder that this King is also the New Testament King Jesus, the "star" of Bethlehem. In my work, blue is the colour of faithfulness. The vivid, deep-blue background behind the gates reminds us of God's unfailing commitment to his promises.

Psalm 24

My head is high, GOD, held high;
I'm looking to you, GOD; . . .

**Show me how you work, GOD;
School me in your ways.**

**Take me by the hand;
Lead me down the path of truth.
You are my Savior, aren't you?**

Mark the milestone of your mercy and love, GOD;
Rebuild the ancient landmarks! . . .

GOD is fair and just;
He corrects the misdirected,
Sends them in the right direction.

He gives the rejects his hand,
And leads them step by step.

From now on every road you travel
Will take you to GOD.
Follow the Covenant signs;
Read the charted directions.

There is a dark maze of roads and tracks here, and it is confusing to find the right way. But God's way, spelt out in the Hebrew letters representing God's name YHWH, is clearly illuminated. It rises, step by step, round sharp bends and with unexpected corners. There is no end to this path—note above, to the right—but it leads to a Future! The word "truth", as it is used in this psalm—doing what is right—is represented by the two engraved stone slabs of God's Law. It is with God's presence—light—and by God's Law—truth—that a person may pick their way safely through the labyrinth of life.

Psalm 25

Light, space, zest—
      that's GOD!
So, with him on my side I'm fearless,
      afraid of no one and nothing. . . .

Listen GOD, I'm calling at the top of my lungs:
      "Be good to me! Answer me!"
When my heart whispered, "Seek God,"
      my whole being replied,
"I'm seeking him!"
      Don't hide from me now!

You've always been right there for me;
      don't turn your back on me now.
Don't throw me out, don't abandon me;
      you've always kept the door open.
My father and mother walked out and left me,
      But GOD took me in.

In the opening verses of this psalm the poet describes the peak times in his life of faith—represented by the green band on the left. In the verses following, which inspired the larger part of this painting, the poet has fallen into depths of despair—black shadows below. The red line shooting out of these dark depths expresses the cry "Be good to me! Answer me, God!" Although God seems to hide himself at times, he allows himself to be found by those who seek him—note the light sphere entering from above, to the right.

Psalm 27

The biblical image of a mountainous rock, a place of safety, fascinates me. The verses of this psalm describe God as solid and secure like a mountain boulder—you can build your life on this rock. In the painting the boulders are composed to point sharply up to heaven. The rock on the right is a solid one and on top of it one can just make out a fortress; God is a safe hiding place. The hollow cave below, in the rock on the left, represents the safe place with God where a person may hide from danger, until the storm is past, and from the heat of the sun.

I run to you, GOD; I run for dear life.
  Don't let me down!
  Take me seriously this time!
Get down on my level and listen,
  and please—no procrastination!
Your granite cave is a hiding place,
  your high cliff aerie a place of safety.

You're my cave to hide in,
  my cliff to climb.
Be my safe leader,
  be my true mountain guide.
Free me from hidden traps;
  I want to hide in you.
I've put my life in your hands.
  You won't drop me,
  you'll never let me down.

Psalm 31

The poet finds himself in exile in the land of the Jordan, of Mount Hermon, the land to the north of Israel. There he remembers— note the added fragment of Plexiglas, a "fragment of the past"—how he used to go up to Jerusalem, to God's Temple, foremost amongst the crowd of worshippers. He cries out as a stab of longing pierces him—see below, on the right. But the psalmist feels rejected by God and by folk, and sorrow, like waves, crushes over his soul—see below, to the left.

A white-tailed deer drinks
    from the creek;
I want to drink God,
    deep draughts of God.
I'm thirsty for God-alive.
I wonder, "Will I ever make it—
    arrive and drink in God's presence?" . . .

These are the things I go over and over,
    emptying out the pockets of my life.
I was always at the head of the worshiping crowd,
    right out in front,
Leading them all,
    eager to arrive and worship,
Shouting praises, singing thanksgiving—
    celebrating, all of us, God's feast! . . .

When my soul is in the dumps, I rehearse
    everything I know of you,
From Jordan depths to Hermon heights,
    including Mount Mizar.
Chaos calls to chaos,
    to the tune of whitewater rapids.
Your breaking surf, your thundering breakers
    crash and crush me.

Psalm 42

Why are you down in the dumps, dear soul?
      Why are you crying the blues?
Fix my eyes on God—
      soon I'll be praising again.
He puts a smile on my face.
      He's my God. . . .

Sometimes I ask God, my rock-solid God,
      "Why did you let me down?
Why am I walking around in tears,
      harassed by enemies?"
They're out for the kill, these
      tormentors with their obscenities,
Taunting day after day,
      "Where is this God of yours?"

Why are you down in the dumps, dear soul?
      Why are you crying the blues?
Fix my eyes on God—
      soon I'll be praising again.
He puts a smile on my face.
      He's my God.

The verse that is pictured here is repeated in Psalm 43:5. The psalmist wants to know why he feels so sad? Why so troubled? His restlessness is expressed in the collage of black and red stained and torn surfaces; he is almost destroyed by the immense pressure pushing him down. But when the psalmist experiences God's liberation—the bright arm intervening to stop his plunge into the darkness—he thankfully praises God, whose presence is marked by gold in the upper section, to the right.

Psalm 42

Be good to me, God—and now!
    I've run to you for dear life.
I'm hiding out under your wings
    until the hurricane blows over.
I call out to High God,
    the God who holds me together.
He sends orders from heaven and saves me,
    He humiliates those who kick me around.
God delivers generous love,
    He makes good on his word.

I find myself in a pride of lions
    who are wild for a taste of human flesh;
Their teeth are lances and arrows,
    their tongues are sharp daggers.

Soar high in the skies, O God!
    Cover the whole earth with your glory!

A vast, light, protecting, winged shape and its shadow dominate this painting. This winged shape represents the safe cover God provides for his people; he covers them until the terror has passed by. The "terror" is expressed as aggressive, sharp, flaming arrows, daggers that pierce. Note also that from behind the shadow the light of the sun is emerging.

Psalm 57

The curved line in the upper part of this painting separates two contrasting planes: one of coloured restlessness—the daily life—and one of bright and peaceful, misty light—the poet's still waiting for God. The rock, which here symbolizes God, is central in the composition and its shape reminds us of a lion. A light, horizontal line depicts the water surface. The relatively small part of the rock protruding above the water surface is no measure of the vast and firm, solid rock base which is hidden from sight underneath the water. So it is with God—when we see only a small part of his work, it is easy to forget that our God is mighty.

God, the one and only—
　　　　I'll wait as long as he says.
Everything I need comes from him,
　　　　so why not?
He's solid rock under my feet,
　　　　breathing room for my soul,
An impregnable castle:
　　　　I'm set for life. . . .

My help and glory are in God
　　　　—granite-strength and safe-harbor-God—
So trust him absolutely, people;
　　　　lay your lives on the line for him.
　　　　God is a safe place to be.

Psalm 62

The poet lives far away and longs to travel to Jerusalem, to the Temple, to be close to God. He thinks of the birds that fly around the Temple grounds, building their nests, even in the Temple pillars. This painting shows the head of one of the pair of copper pillars at the Temple entrance. The pillar was called Boaz (cf. 1 Kings 7:15-22) and had a lily-shaped capital, decorated with a pattern of seven interwoven chains and pomegranate shapes. A space high up in the capital provides a nesting place for the sparrow and the swallow—they can get no closer to God. The sparrow and the swallow are important in this psalm; therefore they appear disproportionately large. They are well camouflaged and blend in with the building so as to live discreetly close to God. The psalmist envies them!

What a beautiful home, GOD of the Angel Armies!
 I've always longed to live in a place like this,
Always dreamed of a room in your house,
 where I could sing for joy to God-alive!

Birds find nooks and crannies in your house,
 sparrows and swallows make nests there.
They lay their eggs and raise their young,
 singing their songs in the place where
  we worship.
GOD of the Angel Armies! King! God!
 How blessed they are to live and sing there! . . .

One day spent in your house, this beautiful place
  of worship,
 beats thousands spent on Greek island beaches.
I'd rather scrub floors in the house of my God
 than be honored as a guest in the palace of sin.
All sunshine and sovereign is GOD,
 generous in gifts and glory.
He doesn't scrimp with his traveling companions.
 It's smooth sailing all the way with GOD of the
  Angel Armies.

Psalm 84

This composition consists of three distinct parts: on the left, life is portrayed as a flower that shoots up from the earth, with vibrant leaves and a colourful bud, almost floating away. The dark middle section shows how trials test life, just as the storms and rain test the strength of the flowering plant. When the flower stem snaps, the flower falls, its leaves dry up, and only a dead twig is left. So too, when a person dies, the memory soon fades of their once-promising life. It seems as if nothing is left behind. But in the area to the right we glimpse the flower continuing to bloom, on into eternity, an image of God's promised gift of eternal life.

GOD is sheer mercy and grace;
    not easily angered, he's rich in love.
He doesn't endlessly nag and scold,
    nor hold grudges forever.
He doesn't treat us as our sins deserve,
    nor pay us back in full for our wrongs.
As high as heaven is over the earth,
    so strong is his love to those who fear him.
And as far as sunrise is from sunset,
    he has separated us from our sins.
As parents feel for their children,
    GOD feels for those who fear him.
He knows us inside and out,
    keeps in mind that we're made of mud.
Men and women don't live very long;
    like wildflowers they spring up and blossom.
But a storm snuffs them out just as quickly,
    leaving nothing to show they were here.
GOD's love, though, is ever and always,
    eternally present to all who fear him,
Making everything right for them and their children
    as they follow his Covenant ways
    and remember to do whatever he said.

Psalm 103

I'm ready, God, so ready,
    ready from head to toe.
Ready to sing,
    ready to raise a God-song:
"Wake, soul! Wake, lute!
    Wake up, you sleepyhead sun!"

I'm thanking you, GOD, out in the streets,
    singing your praises in town and country.
The deeper your love, the higher it goes;
    every cloud's a flag to your faithfulness.
Soar high in the skies, O God!
    Cover the whole earth with your glory!
And for the sake of the one you love so much,
    reach down and help me—answer me! . . .

Give us help for the hard task;
    human help is worthless.
In God we'll do our very best;
    he'll flatten the opposition for good.

Psalm 108

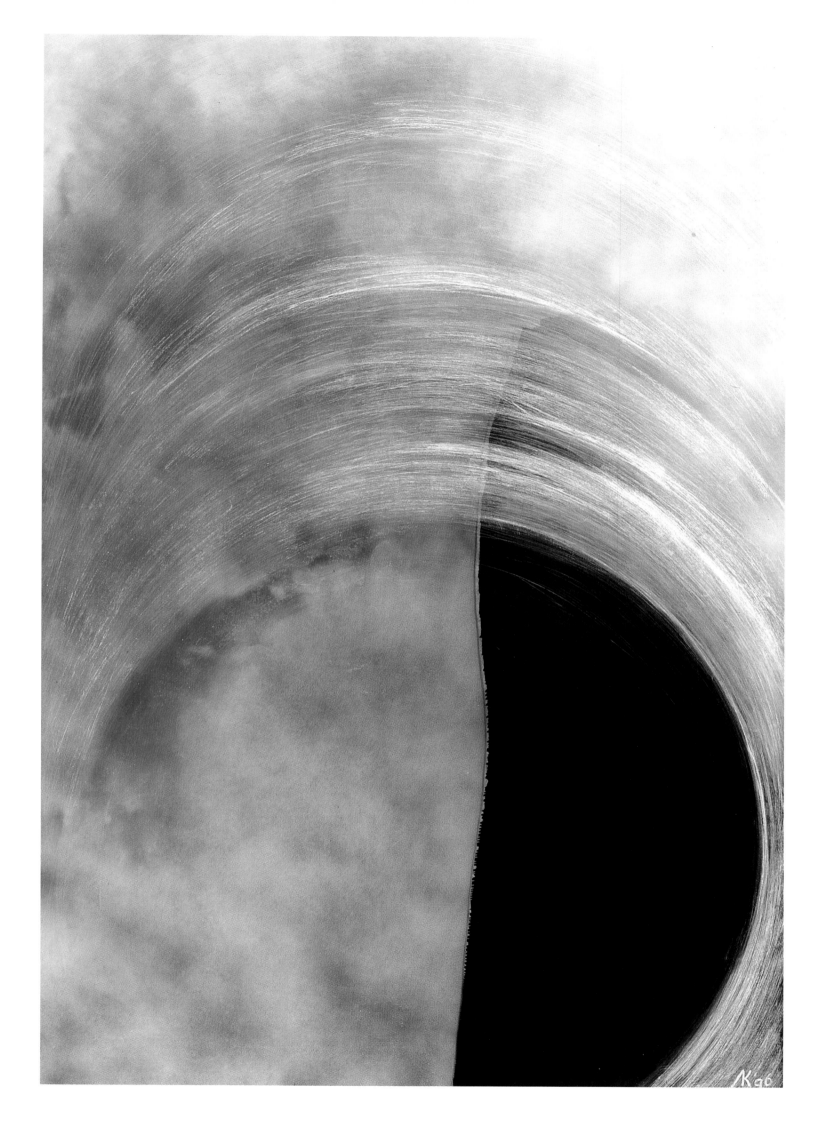

By your words I can see where I'm going;
    they throw a beam of light on my dark path.
I've committed myself and I'll never turn back
    from living by your righteous order.
Everything's falling apart on me, G OD;
    put me together again with your Word.
Festoon me with your finest sayings, G OD;
    teach me your holy rules.
My life is as close as my own hands,
    but I don't forget what you have revealed.
The wicked do their best to throw me off track,
    but I don't swerve an inch from your course.
I inherited your book on living; it's mine forever—
    what a gift! And how happy it makes me!
I concentrate on doing exactly what you say—
    I always have and always will.

The path of life is a rocky road and often leads through the darkness. In this work a torch represents the Word of God, and the beam of light from it clearly shows up the dangers ahead— uneven edges, sharp obstacles jutting out from the rock faces, even shards of broken glass.

Psalm 119

I look up to the mountains;
> **does my strength come from mountains?**
No, my strength comes from GOD,
> **who made heaven, and earth, and mountains.**

He won't let you stumble,
> your Guardian God won't fall asleep.
Not on your life! Israel's
> Guardian will never doze or sleep.

GOD's your Guardian,
> right at your side to protect you—
Shielding you from sunstroke,
> sheltering you from moonstroke.

GOD guards you from every evil,
> he guards your very life.
He guards you when you leave and when you return,
> he guards you now, he guards you always.

The writer of this psalm looks up at the mountains with outstretched arms. Can he find help from there? At the same time God is reaching down to fill the empty, outstretched hands—seen by the curved area of descending light. The depth of the darkness below emphasizes the vast height of the mountain above. But it is from God that help comes, from God who is higher and more trustworthy and secure than the most majestic of mountains!

Psalm 121

The dark-red figure on the right of this painting stands abandoned against the background of a dry desert region. The dark cloud above further threatens this deserted life. But the figure is supported by a bright outline, representing the ever-attentive presence of God, who keeps a person's feet from stumbling. God is so intimately concerned about his people that, all around, behind and in front of them, like a shadow, he never abandons them. Note how the shadow threatens to get left behind, but even then, during the most threatening times of loss, God sticks to his people. The bright outline enfolds the footing of the shadow, protecting the very basis on which the person stands.

I look up to the mountains;
        does my strength come from mountains?
No, my strength comes from GOD,
        who made heaven, and earth, and mountains.

He won't let you stumble,
        your Guardian God won't fall asleep.
Not on your life! Israel's
        Guardian will never doze or sleep.

GOD's your Guardian,
        right at your side to protect you—
Shielding you from sunstroke,
        sheltering you from moonstroke.

GOD guards you from every evil,
        he guards your very life.
He guards you when you leave and when you return,
        he guards you now, he guards you always.

Psalm 121

Those who trust in GOD
        are like Zion Mountain:
Nothing can move it, a rock-solid mountain
        you can always depend on.
Mountains encircle Jerusalem,
        and GOD encircles his people—
        always has and always will.
The fist of the wicked
        will never violate
What is due the righteous,
        provoking wrongful violence.
Be good to your good people, GOD,
        to those whose hearts are right!
GOD will round up the backsliders,
        corral them with the incorrigibles.
Peace over Israel!

Jerusalem is built on seven hills. In the centre of this composition is Mount Moria, where the Temple stood, also called the Temple Mountain. The other six mountains are grouped around Jerusalem. The shape of a circle often represents eternity in symbolic art; God, here represented by a bright circle of light, surrounds his people as the mountains surround Jerusalem. The surrounding mountains join up in the shape of a star, the star of David, to depict the people of Israel. The stark, black outline of the star expresses sorrow for the suffering of God's people.

Psalm 125

Help God—the bottom has fallen out of my life!
    Master, hear my cry for help!
Listen hard! Open your ears!
    Listen to my cries for mercy.

If you, God, kept records on wrongdoings,
    who would stand a chance?
As it turns out, forgiveness is your habit,
    and that's why you're worshiped.

I pray to God—my life a prayer—
    and wait for what he'll say and do.
My life's on the line before God, my Lord,
    waiting and watching till morning,
    waiting and watching till morning.

Oh Israel, wait and watch for God—
    with God's arrival comes love,
    with God's arrival comes generous redemption.
No doubt about it—he'll redeem Israel,
    buy back Israel from captivity to sin.

The psalmist is experiencing a deep crisis; it is like being at the bottom of a dark pit out of which his cry rises to God: "Lord, hear my voice." The restless black lines express the fear that surrounds the psalmist as he waits anxiously for God to come to his rescue. As a night watchman waits for the first signs of day, he waits. Already there is a glimmer of morning light—with God there is deliverance.

Psalm 130

GOD, investigate my life;
　　get all the facts firsthand.
I'm an open book to you;
　　even from a distance, you know
　　　　what I'm thinking.
You know when I leave and when I get back;
　　I'm never out of your sight.
You know everything I'm going to say
　　before I start the first sentence.
I look behind me and you're there,
　　then up ahead and you're there, too—
　　your reassuring presence, coming and going.
This is too much, too wonderful—
　　I can't take it all in!

Is there anyplace I can go to avoid your Spirit?
　　to be out of your sight?
If I climb to the sky, you're there!
　　If I go underground, you're there!
If I flew on morning's wings
　　to the far western horizon,
You'd find me in a minute—
　　you're already there waiting!
Then I said to myself, "Oh, he even sees me
　　in the dark!
　　At night I'm immersed in the light!"
It's a fact: darkness isn't dark to you;
　　night and day, darkness and light,
　　　　they're all the same to you.

Psalm 139

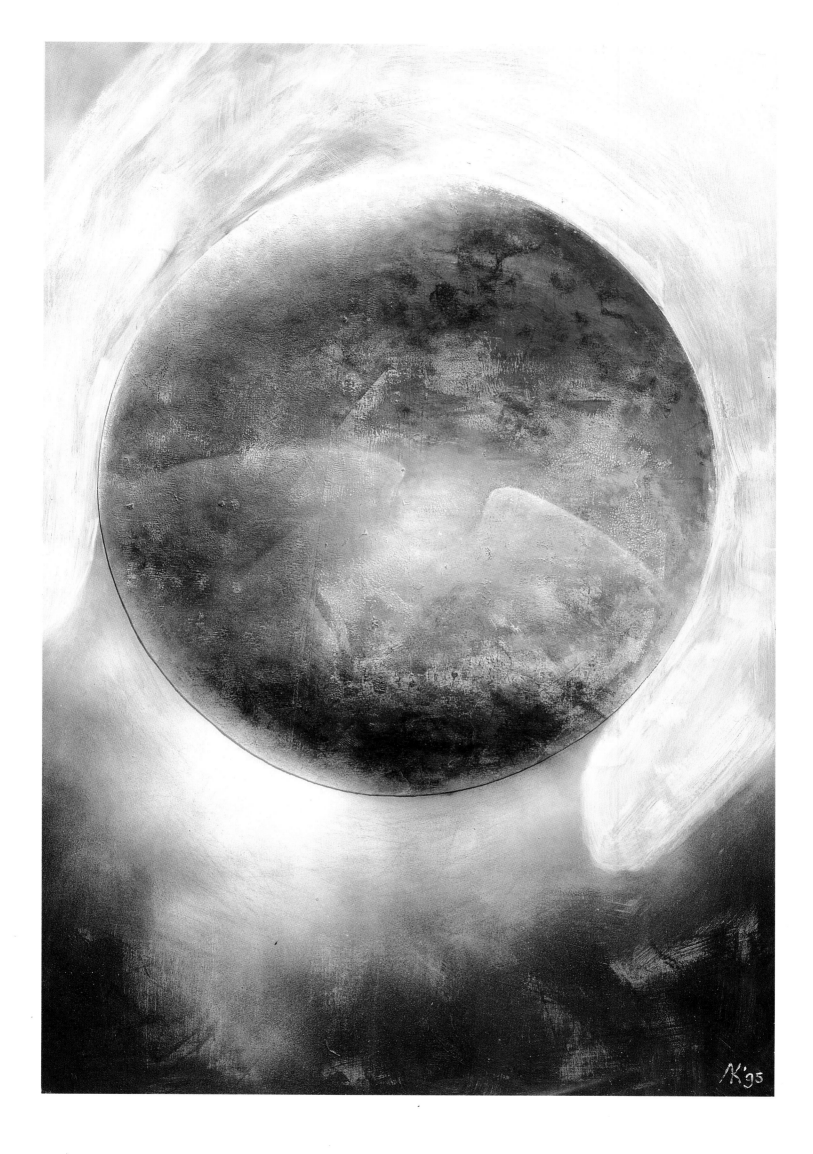

Oh yes, you shaped me first inside, then out;
   you formed me in my mother's womb.
I thank you, High God—you're breathtaking!
   Body and soul, I am marvelously made!
   I worship in adoration—what a creation!
You know me inside and out,
   you know every bone in my body;
You know exactly how I was made, bit by bit,
   how I was sculpted from nothing into
      something.
Like an open book, you watched me grow from
      conception to birth;
   all the stages of my life were spread out
      before you,
The days of my life all prepared
   before I'd even lived one day. . . .

Investigate my life, O God,
   find out everything about me;
Cross-examine and test me,
   get a clear picture of what I'm about;
See for yourself whether I've done anything wrong—
   then guide me on the road to eternal life.

Psalm 139

"I have been made in secret, in the depths of the earth, but all the time you, O God, saw my shapeless beginning," is the deeply moving thought that inspired this work. All attention is centred on the fruit being woven (note the threads), unseen, inside the womb. This is too marvellous for the poet to understand fully, too great and beyond imagining.

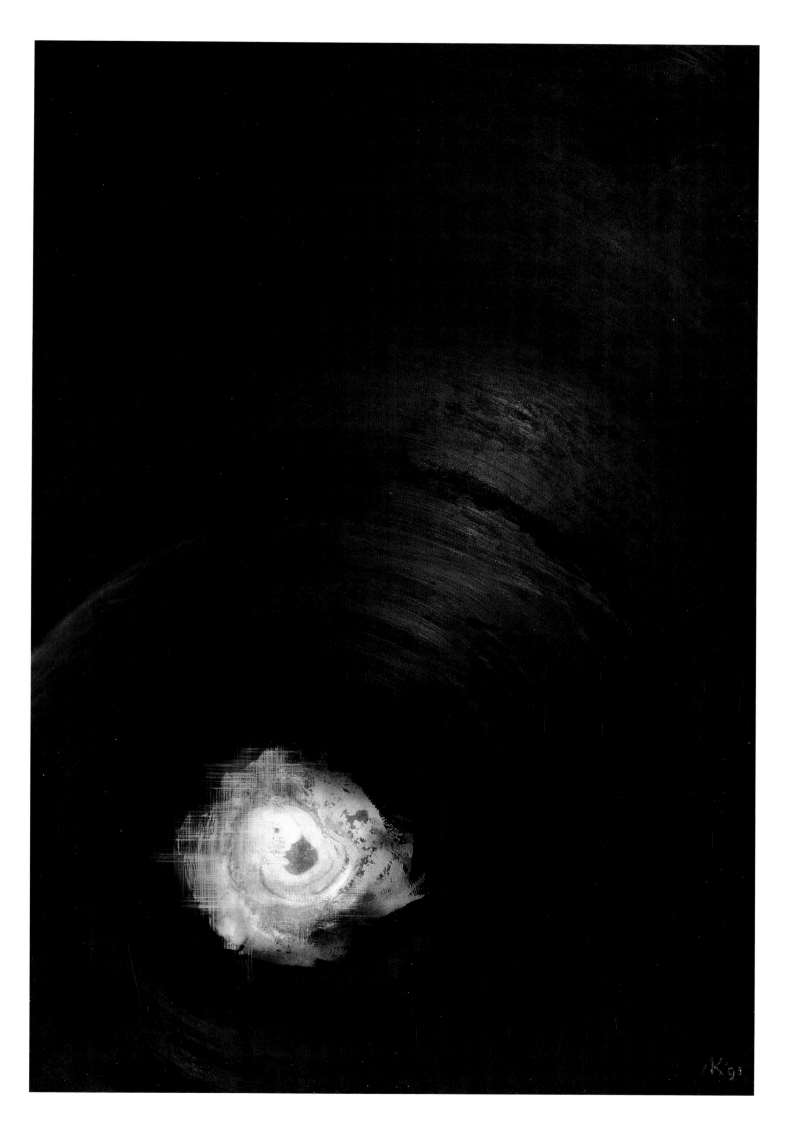

GOD's the one who rebuilds Jerusalem,
    who regathers Israel's scattered exiles.
He heals the heartbroken
    and bandages their wounds.
He counts the stars
    and assigns each a name.
Our Lord is great, with limitless strength;
    we'll never comprehend what he knows
        and does.
GOD puts the fallen on their feet again
    and pushes the wicked into the ditch.

Sing to GOD a thanksgiving hymn,
    play music on your instruments to God,
Who fills the sky with clouds,
    preparing rain for the earth,
Then turning the mountains green with grass,
    feeding both cattle and crows.
He's not impressed with horsepower;
    the size of our muscles means little to him.
Those who fear GOD get GOD's attention;
    they can depend on his strength.

Psalm 147

This is a disturbing painting. It seeks to express what it means to be spiritually totally broken; there is nothing whole in this life. Black and red are emotionally charged colours that give expression to deeply felt pain and suffering, hopelessness and agony. God wants to heal all our brokenness; therefore, and in line with New Testament revelation, the light of God's presence shines through the deep cracks of our shattered brokenness. At the top, to the left, we see the faint shape of the Cross of the Surgeon taking shape through the cracks.

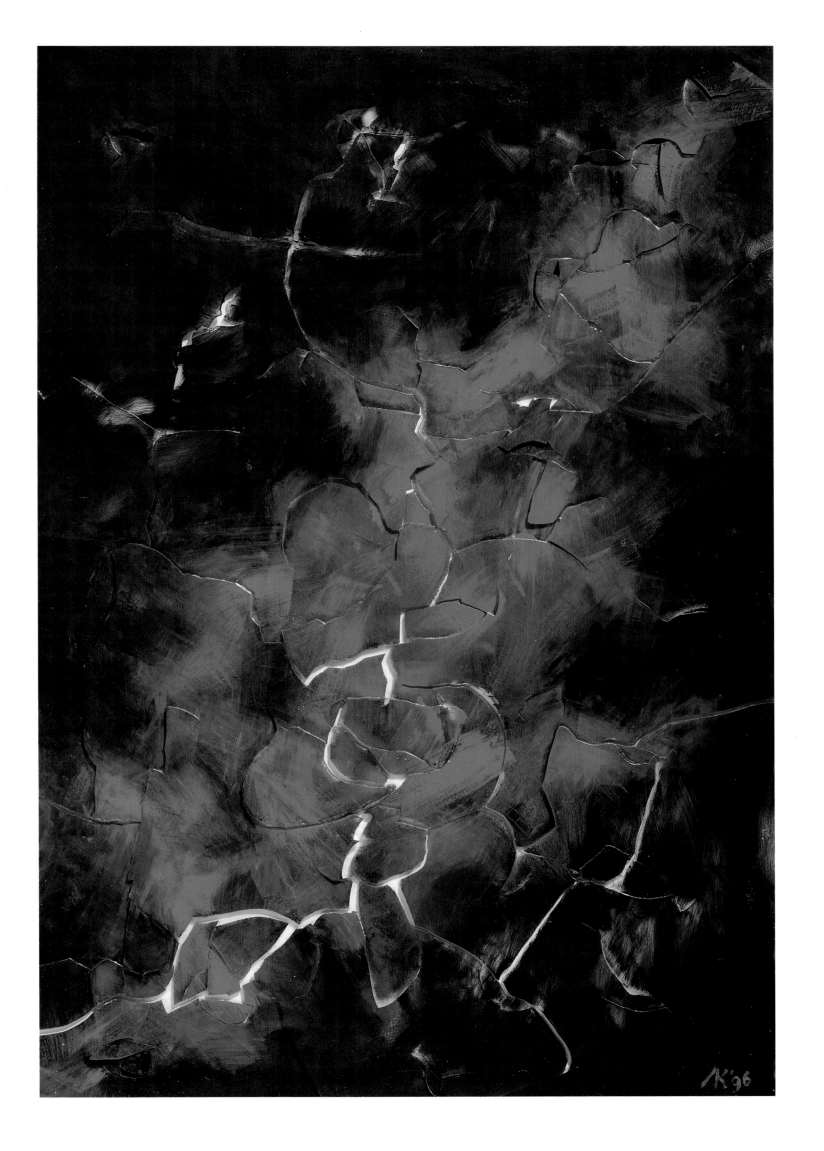

Jerusalem, worship GOD!
Zion, praise your God!
He made your city secure,
he blessed your children among you.
He keeps the peace at your borders,
he puts the best bread on your tables.
He launches his promises earthward—
how swift and sure they come!
He spreads snow like a white fleece,
he scatters frost like ashes,
He broadcasts hail like birdseed—
who can survive his winter?
Then he gives the command and it all melts;
he breathes on winter—suddenly it's
spring!

He speaks the same way to Jacob,
speaks words that work to Israel.
He never did this to the other nations;
they never heard such commands.
Hallelujah!

This is a song of overflowing, total, complete worship, the response of a person who has experienced the omnipotent power of God. The cold colours of the snow, frost and chunks of ice are contrasted with the warm reds that breathe God's love— above, to the left. God's living, warm love conquers the cold, for who could otherwise exist for a single moment! And when that happens, then the water of life flows.

Psalm 147

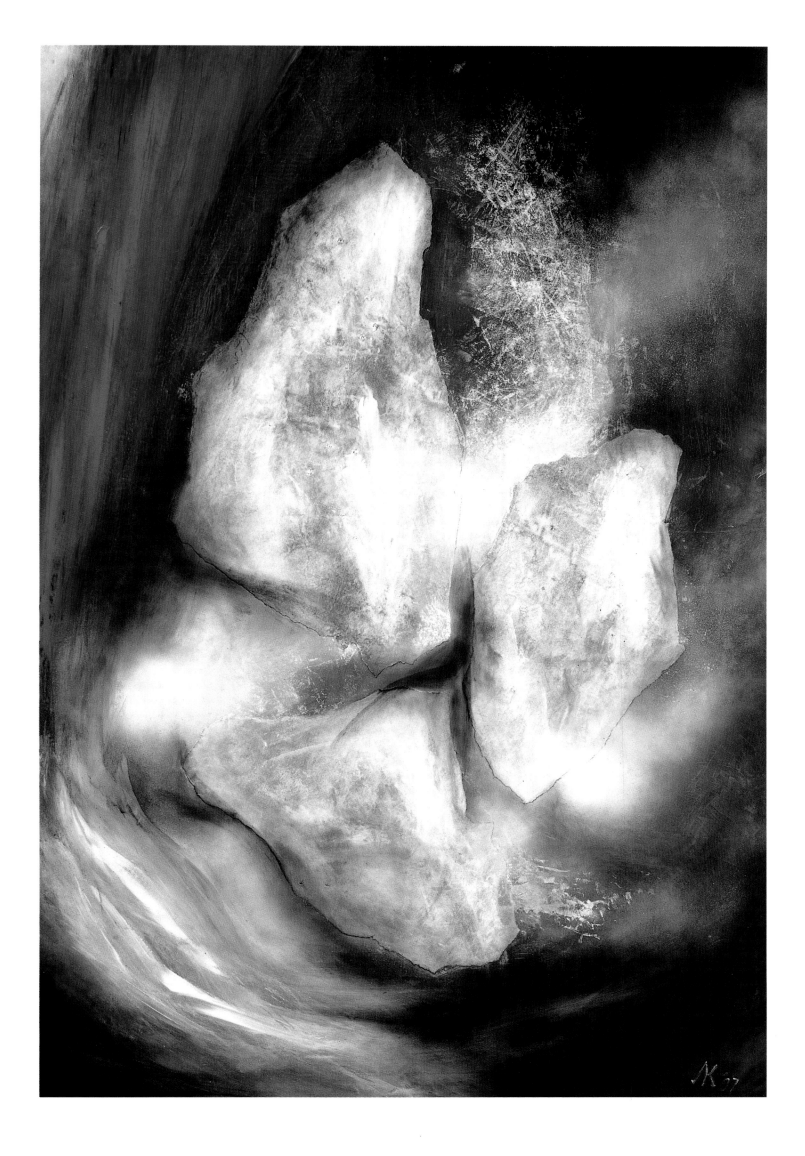

Hallelujah!
Praise God in his holy house of worship,
    praise him under the open skies;
Praise him for his acts of power,
    praise him for his magnificent greatness;
Praise with a blast on the trumpet,
    praise by strumming soft strings;
Praise him with castanets and dance,
    praise him with banjo and flute;
Praise him with cymbals and a big bass drum,
    praise him with fiddles and mandolin.
Let every living, breathing creature praise GOD!
    Hallelujah!

This last psalm radiates a joyful occasion of celebration as all creatures join to express their overwhelming praise for their Creator. Up above in the heavens, God is represented in an abstract manner by arms that lovingly surround the earth. Down below, all the musical instruments listed in this song of praise are gathered together into a colourful, dynamic composition; and breath from the worshipping crowd of human and animal creatures rises up to praise God. Hallelujah!

Psalm 150

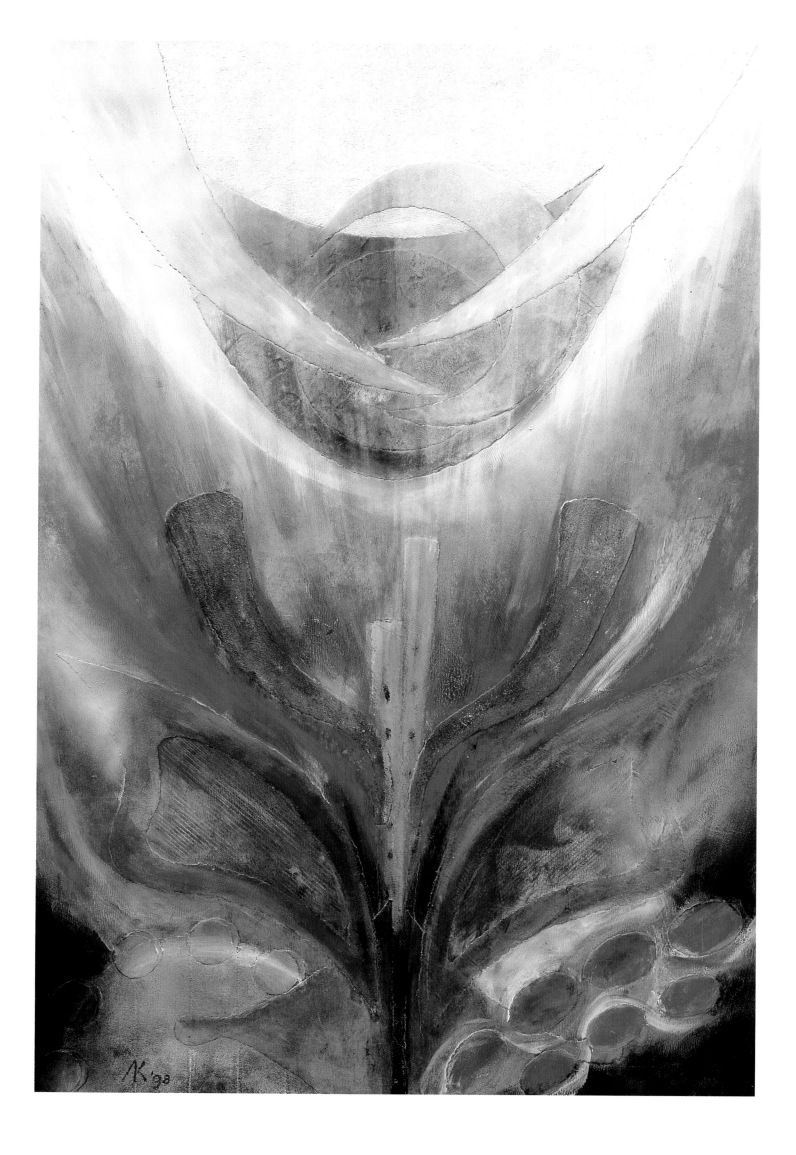